Sightings

Twenty-One Poems Observed

To Caleb —
Fellow Artist!
Hope you enjoy
these poems.
Thanks
A K Steffen
12/13/14

Printed and Published by
Greyden Press

Copyright © 2014 by Cindy K. Steffen

All rights reserved. This book or any portion thereof may not be reproduced or used in any manner whatsoever without the express written permission of the publisher except for the use of brief quotations in a book review or scholarly journal.

First Printing: 2014

ISBN 978-1-57074-105-0

Printed and Published by
Greyden Press, LLC
2251 Arbor Boulevard
Dayton, OH 45439

For my Father -
who taught me to love nature.

For Craig -
who wraps me always in unconditional love.
You are my gift and my healing.

Author's Note

I wrote most of these poems upon inspiration at Prairie Pond Woods, the retreat property my husband and I own in southern Ohio. A few other poems were written at local preserves or gardens, or while attending a nature journaling workshop in the Berkshires. All photographs were taken by me.

I never set out to write a poem. I only set out to take walks. The poetry comes when I'm present, but lost, in nature. If I'm paying attention, a strong opening line or other phrase darts into my mind, seemingly from out of nowhere. But they are not from out of nowhere. I believe these inspirations are gifts from nature, sometimes from myself, and always from the Creator.

I hope you enjoy reading them as much as I did observing them.

Be still…bear fruit,

Cindy K. Steffen

Table of Contents

I Am 1

Spring

Timepieces 3
Guilder's Pond 5
Twilight Song 7
A Poem of Questions 8
One Walk 11

Summer

Lake Katherine 12
Spider 14
Neighbor's Garden 16
Sora 19
Butterfly Watching 21

Fall

October Morning 23
Holy Ground 25
At Twilight 27
Old Bones / Old Souls 28
Ode to Old 31

Winter

What Speaks Beneath 32
December 18 35
Wondering 36
Teacher 39

The Gardener 40

I Am

    Keeper of lonely places
    Of beauty
    Of the quiet fog
    On the contoured land,
    Friend of seekers
    Of hearts in wonder
    Hearts dry from routine,
    Color-watcher and Archivist
    Sharing soft spots to land
    Grassy fields
    Down comforters
    Circles of Souljourners,
    Offering solitude in waiting
    Mindfulness to dream,
    Path-Walker and Collector
    Home-maker of host plants
    Cups of healing tea and rest,
    Packing dirt and field journals
    Co-laborer, am I

TIMEPIECES

This rock, compressed sea upon ancient sea,
crowned the surface over a million years ago.

Fissures, cutting and prying for centuries,
segment the face like the wrinkles of a corpse.

The talus, broken off before Darwin was born,
migrates, inch by inch, down the slope.

Patches of moss return each year, covering
more and more surface, like suburbs after the war.

Seeds of the columbine anchored firmly in
a crevice, when Dylan sang of wind & answers.

Water drips from cracks like sweat,
seeking light and earth since winter's melt.

A spider, patient inside a tiny opening,
will not make it through the summer.

Its prey, with only days to live then die,
emerged just yesterday.

This morning a hiker passed
and asked what time it was.

MORNING AT GUILDER'S POND

Surrounded by firs, pink kalmia
and tannic water the color of motor oil,
I drop my pack.
I can go no further on this rocky trail.

Perhaps, if I were braver –
this gray, rotted bridge has surrendered
only its middle to the pond.
I could leap. I choose to sit.

Am I too old to try to cross?
Perhaps this is just a perfect place
to yield and let what lies beyond
remain a mystery.

I glide my binoculars in a semi-circle.
The beaver dam that hides me
rests against an old, cracked foundation.
Together they hold the water back.

The pond shimmers at eye level,
like double-paned glass reflecting
light off the still surface and
on to the layer of life skimming above it.

I stand to leave.
Angles of sunlight shift and
the top sheet shatters.
Only shards made of dragonflies remain.

TWILIGHT SONG

      Evening shadow falls heavily over the
      last birds calling, as if the black lid of a
      grand piano slowly closes over its strings.

      Their songs, fading in the dusk,
      trail sweetly from the trees, then
      hush, as the Wood Thrush begins its solo.

      They perform no finale' at twilight.
      That grand end they leave to the stars,
      silent and spread against a dark velvet curtain.

      Orchestras bowing in their seats.

A POEM OF QUESTIONS

A friend says I should write poetry again.
It's been awhile. There's been death,
discouragement,
flooding,
regime changes,
shear laziness.
And who am I or what do I have to say?
And would the reader care?
Is there a poem to write
that would touch
or transform anyone?

The old adage is: write what you know.

Do I write about the gnarly sycamore tree
which, though it dons a camouflage cover,
is always spotted
where water
baptizes its roots?

Do I describe Pink Lady's Slipper orchids,
whose ironic, masculine form springs only from soil
made acid by
worn sandstone,
broken shale,
time?

Should the poem ask the reader,
"Did you know you can read the land this way?"
But who cares, really? Isn't land just for
buying and selling,
building upon,
and harvesting from?

Are words wasted when a poem beckons readers
(aren't people too busy for poetry?)
to reflect
on a park bench,
a trail,
or a bridge above
a lyrical stream?

Could the poem invite them to stop listening,
just for those rare, few moments
to the voices of culture,
of family,
or the lies,
we tell
ourselves,
and listen only to the song of the red-eyed vireo,
high in the forested canopy
chanting his mnemonic mantra?

"See me" "Up here." "Here I am"

Can a poem, even a silly one, inspire?
Might someone read it, then stand barefoot
on spongy grass,
rotting leaves,
hard, hewn wood,
and raise their golden face,
hands open to the sun,
or the black, rolling clouds,
to a slice of moon,
and shout,
maybe for the first time,

"See me! Down here! Here I am!"

ONE WALK

One dog
One woman
One singular path
One solitary place
One fetid deer carcass
One song of the wood thrush
One vernal creek barely flowing
One and only one columbine bloom
One transient red-winged blackbird
One smile thinking of a friend's visit
One tick lying-in-wait for our breath
One monotonous drill of a sapsucker
One ventriloquist song of the ovenbird
One sunlit and streaked prairie warbler
One green heron scared up at the pond
One gobble-gobble from the hills beyond
One nose sniffing out all manner of stench
One "Thinking of You" card in the mailbox
One phoebe nest fabricated on the shutter
One patch of planted ephemerals flourishing
One honeysuckle seed, germinated and grown
One tree yanked down and strangled by its vine
One sessile trillium where none had been before
One hope that joy and sacrifice meet, and the world is saved.

LAKE KATHERINE

Sitting on this log I can't see
the steep plunge of the falls
but I can feel the sound from below,
filling the gorge with white-water noise.
"Just listen," I tell myself.

Later on the rumbling bridge,
the water scouring below me,
I think about the lesson I just learned –

Never go 'round a bend too quickly
or you will miss the blue heron
rising from the bottom of the falls.

Vulture shadows glide across trees,
fooling me to look up every time.
"Be still and wait."
What comes is a water thrush, tail
bobbing, searching for food along the
rusted shores of the little eddy.

How could that dragonfly have
been so slow? Swallowed whole.
Only glittering pieces of delicate
wing left behind.

"Remember the heron," I say,
doubling back towards the trailhead.
Silent at the turn, I spot a kingfisher
and watch it,
perched still and forgiving, on a dead,
weathered tree in Lake Katherine.

SPIDER

After Friends,
we both come
out into the thick,
August air, only
slightly cooler than
before the nightly news

Barely on the porch,
she drops before me,

like a Navy Seal, and
performs her orb dance -

Eight legs, frantic and
not one is tangled,
for twenty minutes and
twenty inches round.

She is an artist,
an inspiration,
a nun, praying the
silken rosary.
She is hungry.

Tomorrow I will forget.
When the dog needs out
I will walk face first into it,
cursing

By then, she will have
woven a mystery, captured
prey and <u>survived victorious</u>.

I will have barely strung
sentences together
on this page
and pee'd the dog.

NEIGHBOR'S GARDEN

    I come to pick up vacation mail,
    And suddenly I am on a safari.

    Morning breezes usher out the haze;
    Now open-stage for all winged creatures -

    Black vulture and hummingbird,
    Monarch and Viceroy twin.

Pearl Crescents, lost among black-eyed Susans,
rise like a wave when the wind stirs.

A dragonfly charges me, defending its prey.
Odd, seeing the tables turned on a yellow jacket.

All around me, movement, like random leaves
letting go from an early autumn frost.

There are no fragrances this late in summer,
only the thick smell of heat rising.

Din of August music ebbs and flows and ebbs;
faint background static of cicadas.

But there is no shortage of color-
soaring,
gliding,
fluttering,
basking,
launching and landing-

I'd go deaf if I could hear their wing beats.

SORA

The Sora looked foolish enough,
flapping up from the cattails and
staggering in front of me, like a drunk,
across the boardwalk.

In an instant, it sliced through tall reeds,
vanishing in the swallow of the marsh,
a wake of bright green confetti
closing up behind it.

First amused, then gripped by a sad curiosity -
like an adolescent boy wanting just a peep -
I yearn to know this beautiful, elusive creature.
Yet I am an alien and unwelcome here.

In the mystery of this ancient exchange -
to hear the pitch of unfamiliar calls,
smell air's perfume, touch earth's moist skin -
we can only offer our muted senses.

All that ever shouts or echoes back is fear.

BUTTERFLY WATCHING

        Like flower-heads popping off their stems
        To Float willy-nilly on the fickle lift of wind –

        Eastern Blue Tails or Violets?
        Red-spotted Purples or Iris?
        Clouded Sulfers or Buttercups?
        Frittalaries or Poppies?
        Who can say?

        How wonderful to gather a mixed bouquet
        and place on my nightstand, so all that
        fluttering would lull my mind to sleep.

        Then every morning release them to the sun,
        and every evening set off down the trail
        with a fresh vase of stems.

OCTOBER MORNING

The Eastern Towhee sings a two-syllable chirp
in the silver maple near the deck, as the
sleepy, gray dawn slowly brightens, then sparks,
igniting quiet into cacophonies

Each bird's rhythm joins together – four crow caws,
five quick buzzes from the titmouse, the never ending
screech of a blue jay, two electric bubbles from
bluebirds on wires, toy-squeaks from a flicker
- calling to the world, each other, to God,
that their life matters.

Would that we might wake up each morning and
scream for hours from our porches - who we are,
our intentions, the names of those we love and our
new one, if God re-named us like the Sons of Thunder.

By mid-morning the measured calls start to wane.
Sounds of the human day begin – a chained dog barks,
cars chase each other down appointed routes,
in the distance, the growl of machinery.

Later when daily chores are behind me,
I'll sit and listen to their choruses again,
chattering in the trees as they store up seed
at the feeder for the long, chilly night ahead.

Their voice, my voice, your voice fills the world.

HOLY GROUND

We struck a bargain this past spring,
or rather,
we struck a secret bargain when you left the
newly-planted mountain laurel gnarly and leafless,
and stripped small oaks of their budding futures.

You will eat the dirty, orange persimmons
fallen from the lichen-covered tree on the hill.
Though you left us only four to gather all season,
to taste their pungent flesh, we don't mind.

You will eat the bruised and misshapen apples
further up the hill, too full of blackberry canes to
make it worth the climb. If you dare glean them in
the barbed thicket, we're happy to share.

You will walk our mowed paths through the prairie
and bed down at the edge under spreading pines.
You will drink from the secluded pond, lick the salt
and lay hidden in the bluestem beneath the evening sun.

Then, after the fall equinox and first full moon - the Terms.

We will stand over your muscled body with graceful
eyes and recall our encounters, evanescent and awful.
We will thank you and then give thanks, knowing the ground
we stand on, blood-soaked and bargained for, is holy.

AT TWILIGHT

The scooped-out moon rests its crescent tip
on the low-strung wire from an old mercury light,
disconnected so no moths and birds are confused
and no stars polluted when sun and moon trade shifts.

My dog lays in the yard chewing a bone she can barely see;
the vertebrae of a deer carcass sniffed out in the cedars,
pranced down the trail like spoils of war in her mouth.
Content on the front porch in this dusky, gray hue,
I watch, listen, and sniff the cool air like she does.

Our neighbor died in early summer. Her son moved to
the white farmhouse where he grew up and will grow old.
He hammers in this low light, finishing up the wood shed
begun first thing in the heat, knowing what country folk know.

There is hardly a care for what people think these days -
what I look like, what I do, what I believe.
There is only a deep care that I make a difference,
now that I know who I am.

The first half trading places with the second half;
this is the curiosity and peace of a life at twilight.

OLD BONES / OLD SOULS

>Lots of crunching and cracking
>interrupt this quiet fall morning-
>the kind of perfect day I wish
>would hold in every cell of my body.
>
>But it's not just my old bones I hear,
>it's the twig-snap of a white-tailed deer
>running scared when the path turns.

It's the squirrels making provisions,
their chins char-colored from
gleaning black, cracked walnuts.

It's the blue jay, high in the canopy
hammering hickory nuts and letting
the pieces splatter to the dry ground.
It's hundreds of grackles and blackbirds,
chattering as they migrate en masse
from one tree top to another, then disappear.

Their chorus, which is for my education,
(they know how to navigate this change),
comforts and reminds me; "It's time...
...to get ready
...to wind down
...to make soup
...to have some folks over
...to learn something new,
on those too-soon nights
when the wind threatens harm
outside the frosted window."

"Study blackbirds" they're suggesting.
This is what those old souls are clacking.
They're reminding me what I forget each year-
That there is time enough, and sacred purpose
for every season

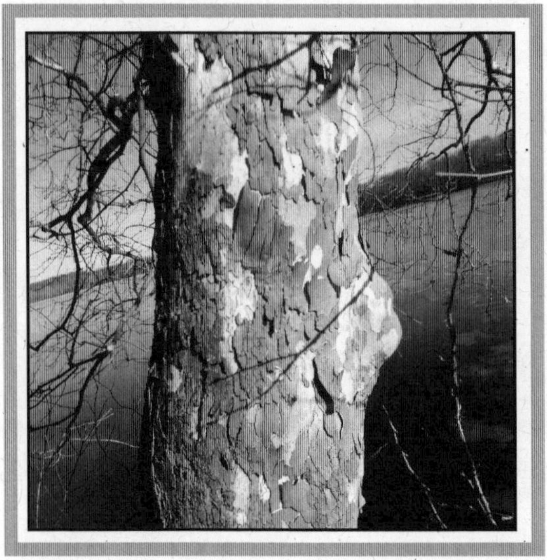

ODE TO OLD

When I am old I won't wear purple or red,
For those are the colors of royalty and harlots.
Since I am neither, (as of this writing)
I will not start the practice then.

No, I will wear the deep hues of brown and green,
and the faded rust of last year's leaves.
Because I am, after all, slowly exiting back to earth
with every breath and birthday bow.

On my 80th, I'll buy hunting camo
and walk daily, briskly as I can, through the woods,
hoping for one last sighting of fall mushrooms
before my heart hopefully gives out.

At 90 I'll don the September outfit again
but only on blustery days, to sit reminiscent
and waiting beneath large, hollow sycamores,
with precariously hanging branches.

At 95, if all that exercise has kept me too
long on this side of the veil, I'll walk
naked, finally, into the forest of turning trees-
to a place filled with colors no one has imagined.

WHAT SPEAKS BENEATH

    Under the piles of artful leaves in these woods,
    under the leaves-turned-soil, above the deeper
    dirt of a millennia of leaf litter, there may be a gold
    wedding ring lying cool and cushioned in the dark.

    Once lost, perhaps after a young man with sore
    muscles and a blister coming on laid it
    foolishly on a freshly sawn stump and forgot it.

Or a young girl, with a name like Imogene or Durinda,
or one we can barely read on old sandstone markers,
threw it at a tree in heart-broken rage and walked away

There are icons of stories below us – beads, wooden
handles, arrowheads that missed and bullets
that hit their mark, coins jostled from pockets, and the
bones of everyone who was loved at least once.

The soil itself lives as an icon of what was – before
we walked here – an ancient oak struck by lightening,
hosting millions of species in life and in death, until it
no longer resemble anything but a rich pile of humus.

No one will know how important that tree was, that
lightening strike, those caterpillars, the birds
foraging there before long migrations, that little
sapling finally growing taller, stronger in the clearing.

Reach down. Kneel down. Smell the wet leaves.
Dig and lift the soil to your face. Breathe in deeply
what the leaves have given us for so long. And listen.
The soil will tell you whatever story you need to hear.

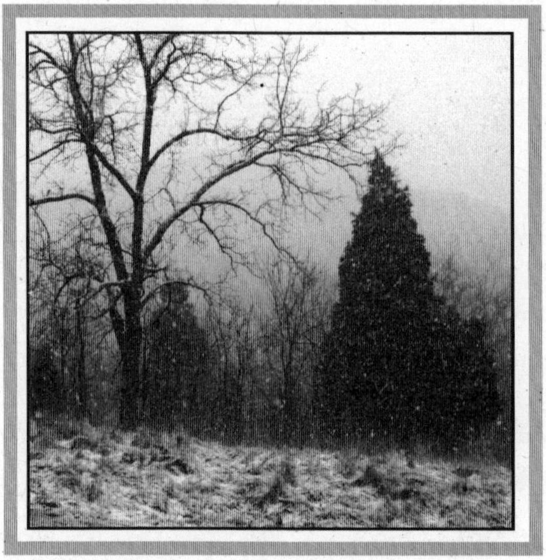

DECEMBER 18

Today I must be filled.

Today I must let the
ornamental pin cherry,
with its birdfeeder swaying
and the rude Downy
selfishly guarding seed,
gently distract.

Today I must walk,
letting the heavy December
snow fall on my forehead,
melt on my glasses,
and not care.

Tomorrow is a beast.
Yesterday I was slain.
Today I am emptied.

Come with me,
my old companion,
let's loosen our bones
on the cold trail.
Walk ahead as you do
sniffing out your world.

I hope you catch the scent of a meadow vole
I hope I catch the fragrance of my life.

WONDERING

    Much rain and the first December cold snap
    left waters overflowing and glazed slick,
    on this day when the sun, a total stranger,
    finally showed its fiery face from dawn to dusk

    The frozen marsh, dotted with flotsam and jetsam,
    jutting trunks and faraway ducks, reflects the sky,
    recently laundered and spread tight, like a plain, blue sheet.

Life and death suspend together here, locked-in
at the edge of these icy waters. And I wonder
how life does its miraculous carrying-on
under this thick, glass ceiling, under the cold mud,
under the rotting logs half-submerged.

Only oak and beech trees rustle their leafy instruments,
hailing me down the trail of littered leaves, alone.
An historical marker tells me this wetland
was once a fur trading business. And I wonder
how different the land before all that blood and commerce.

Cardinals, like fallen clusters of red, ripe berries,
drink from melting puddles up ahead. And I wonder
how something so distinct and vivid can be
taken for granted, as it flies around our yards
and picks at the salt by the side of the road.

And the two brilliant bluebirds, so out of place
in this brown and gray landscape, yet so
perfectly placed for me to see, make me wonder;
Who tells these delicate, feather-painted creatures
to stay for the harshness of winter?

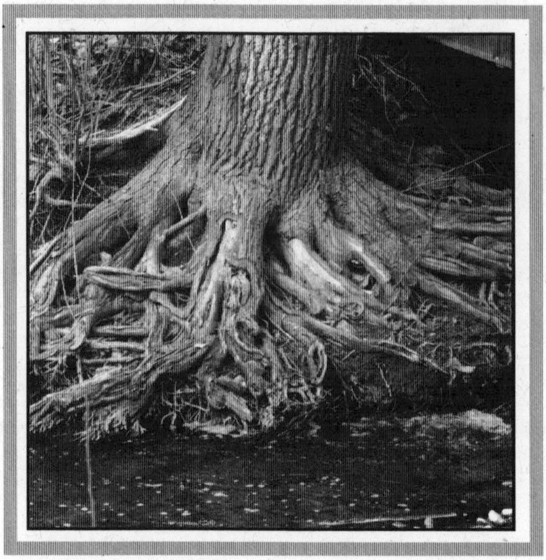

TEACHER

Standing by the creek
grateful that for a time
it is just me and the
soft snow floating alone,

the heron teaches me again
to notice, and expect from any
ordinary moment, a flash of
breathtaking joy.

Wing-thrusts on air whisper beside me,
as I walk along this creek I come to
everyday thinking I am alone.

Turning, it soars past me
through the sentinels of trees
from downstream, where
I had just looked, but did not see.

THE GARDENER

It is fitting that we should crumble your body
and cast it like fertilizer into the ground,
into this earth you could never leave fallow,
though you shook off the dust
from your family farm, never to return.

You, who left young and ambitious
to be a soldier, kept planting and harvesting.
For decades, between three wars, two businesses,
and one marriage, you brought us dirt-laden
lettuce, full bounty and good health.

How will I remember you?
Not the way you hoped, I know.
The veteran and hero of three wars
will always be a warrior in the garden to me,
battling bugs and squirrels and blackbirds.

Because I was not there when you flew
your missions or received your military honors;
I was home with the sitter eating fish sticks
and fighting with my brothers.

But I was there, hot in the backyard, chucking pink
kernels into long rows and kicking them covered.
Together, we exhumed whole potatoes in the fall,
from the halves we laid to rest in summer.

I was there, reluctantly bending to pick beans,
or scratching green-tinted arms covered with the
smell and itch of weighty tomato stems. I would have
rather been with my friends...learning nothing.

I was there later, as you grew tired and solitary,
when you walked slowly out of the garden's heat.
We sat a spell in the shade, sharing a cold drink and
talking about regrets I could not help you forget.

I was there,
when you planted in me my love for the earth,
and all that comes from it.